Happy
Today

Happy Today

Finding Peace and Happiness in the Midst of Your *Everyday Life*

STEVE HAVERLY

HAPPY TODAY
FINDING PEACE AND HAPPINESS IN THE
MIDST OF YOUR EVERYDAY LIFE

iUniverse books may be ordered through booksellers or by contacting:

iUniverse
1663 Liberty Drive
Bloomington, IN 47403
www.iuniverse.com
1-800-Authors (1-800-288-4677)

ISBN: 978-1-4917-6369-8 (sc)
ISBN: 978-1-4917-6370-4 (e)

Library of Congress Control Number: 2015905903

Print information available on the last page.

iUniverse rev. date: 5/27/2015

The information provided in this book is offered in a format of advice and suggestions based on the personal experience and knowledge Steve Haverly has gained through leadership positions in firefighting, martial arts, and church government, in addition to learning from his mentors. He is not a professional psychiatrist or counselor, and this book should in no way be used to treat anyone suffering from a medically diagnosed condition of depression, anxiety, or medically diagnosed disorders. Biblical scriptures are taken from the New International Version unless otherwise noted.

Acknowledgement

To my wife Bobbi:
You are my everything in this world.
Through thick and thin, thank you for
always remaining at my side.
I couldn't do it without you.

Preface

Throughout life, it may be unclear exactly where we're going. I didn't set out in life to write a book, but through the peaks and valleys of the journey, this is where the path led me. Philosophy and concept have always interested me and, I suppose, that has been a catalyst for me to pursue writing about living. Traveling through life, you see many things; maybe more than you wanted to. If you aren't learning something from your experiences then perhaps you are missing something quite beneficial.

I have had the opportunity to lead and follow during my time with several organizations, including professional firefighting, church leadership, and martial arts. My wife Bobbi and I also have helped couples enhance and restore their marriages. This is what I've done and where I've been. And I've seen how all of the challenges during those activities would attempt to steal my peace and joy. I began to learn how I should deal with those problems.

In the past few years, while discussing personal trials that some of my friends were facing, occasionally they would say, "you should write a book." Finally, I decided to compile the thoughts and principles I have used to get, maintain, and grow my personal happiness. I pray that these ideas help you in your life's journey too. Happiness doesn't just happen; it must be cultivated. Allow me to help you begin today.

Contents

Introduction

Have peace. Release stress. Be happy.

Who doesn't want to be happy?
It's something you strive for all your life. When we're young we believe we always will be. In the bliss of our youth everything seems so simple. Happiness just happens every day.

At that time, we have no knowledge that tells us it won't be that way forever. We don't understand things in our youth like death, bills, worry, conflict, work, relationships, pressures, health, and the like. If only we could retain that type of outlook; however, we all know that with time comes experience, maturity, and the uncomfortable understanding of life that slowly erodes the beauty of that youthful innocence.

As growing children, we encounter more and more unpleasant things in between all that fun, such as being "forced" to eat our vegetables, pick up our toys, obey our parents, and other "horrible" things. At that stage in life, those are still momentary awful interruptions in, still, pretty much, fun times.

It doesn't take too long to start seeing life as a list of things that need to be done. Adolescence now has us doing things we're obligated to do, like turning in homework on time, showing up for practice, and doing chores at home.

Then there are the social aspects, such as appearing to fit in with your peers, getting a date, being accepted by the "right" people. Remember? Adolescence is not an easy period of life. Still, though, we find enough time for good experiences through sports, dating, recreation with friends, and so on.

Then in adulthood, life changes as career, spouse, family, home ownership and vehicle maintenance take priority. Raising children is a full-time job in itself. With the other added responsibilities, you can see how making time for yourself and relaxation is pushed into the background.

Pretty soon a pattern sets in: wake up, go to work, come home, do chores, take care of the family and go to bed.

On and on it goes.

The occasional holiday or vacation comes, and we treasure those moments; but all too quickly it's back to the routine. This is a dangerous pattern. Often a person falls into a rut in life thinking it will change or get better, until something snaps inside. When they feel they can't live like this any longer, he or she may take risks or do something out of character like have an extra-marital affair, quit a career, or move to another town with no clear direction. Irrational actions can change life drastically and quickly, and can be very damaging in the long run.

As you read this book, I hope to bring you some insight into how you can live with happiness in your life on a regular basis. I want you to see life clearly and be at peace with it daily. Time is not money. Time is your life. If you spend it being agitated and worried, then your life will be unpleasant. If you spend it at peace and whole, then your life will be just that: peaceful and completely whole.

The everyday is what life is primarily made of, not vacations and Christmas. Let me show you some things I have learned that have changed my life, that I know you can use to change yours, too.

Have peace. Release stress. Be happy.

Chapter 1
Change

Imagine paths around you, leading
away in different directions.

There is a saying I've heard several people quote that I believe is quite powerful, including evangelist and teacher Dr. Mike Murdock, of Fort Worth, Texas, who said, "If you want something you never had, you've got to do something you've never done." It seems so simple, yet many people who want their lives to be different keep living it in the same manner day after day.

To clarify, renowned physicist Albert Einstein is credited with saying "The definition of insanity is to keep doing the same thing, but expecting different results." It's like a stimulus and reaction: if I pinch your arm, you jerk it away. Generally speaking, if I keep pinching your arm over and over, you're not going to eventually giggle as if I were tickling you. You will still pull your arm away. It will require a different kind of stimulus to produce a different reaction.

Few people enjoy change. It's often a difficult process at best. I've chosen to discuss change first because understanding it is going to be important for your progress toward living your life with happiness and contentment.

Now, please don't throw this book down and stomp off thinking this is just another guy who won't let me be myself. It's just another person who thinks I need to be someone I'm not! No, no, no. Relax. That's not my intention. What I'm getting at here is what the great martial artist Bruce Lee referred to as "emptying your cup."

As a martial artist, I have studied Lee and found what many people may not know: Bruce Lee was a great philosopher. He had wisdom about life beyond his 32 short years. He told a story about an English professor who wanted to meet a certain Zen master to learn about his views on life. Upon arriving at the master's home and greeting him, the English professor began a conversation. The professor quickly turned to his own thoughts on life, at which time the master interrupted him, asking the professor if he would like some tea. The professor nodded and went on and on detailing his views. The master set the tray down and began to pour the professor's cup. It filled, ran over and out onto the table. Talking all the while, the professor suddenly shouted "Stop! No more will go in!" The Zen master calmly replied "You are like this cup of tea. You came here saying you wanted to hear my viewpoints, but you are so full of your own ideas that no more will go in. Empty your cup so that it may be filled." (Hyams, 1979)

At this stage, it is important to empty the cup of your mind so that what you learn you considered fully and not immediately dismiss, like the tea running out onto the table.

Consciously open your thoughts to ideas and mental processes that you haven't previously. Changing things in your life begins with changing things in your mind.

To paraphrase Proverbs, as a man thinks in his heart, so is he. (23:7) Your life will go where your mind will go. I'm not trying to force your mind open. Just relax your mind and heart, and be receptive to the thoughts that come your way as you read. This is a huge key to unlocking your newfound contentment with living.

Now is the time

The beginning then, is to make your thoughts open to change, first in your thinking, eventually in your attitudes, and then in your behavior. This will ultimately change your life and the way you feel.

Make a resolution that *now* is the time to do that. Tomorrow won't be any better. Right *now* is the best time. The greatest journey starts with the first step, but that step must be taken; without it, the best travel plans are only a figment of your imagination.

You have to start. The time is now to have an open mind; free to consider, at least, the possibility of change in any or all areas of life. The easiest and most immediate progress you can make is to declare to yourself now: "*I will open my mind to new thoughts and principles that I have never considered. I will look at things that I have already known with renewed openness and without prejudice or opinion.*" There will be plenty of time later to form firm ideas.

Please understand: when the opportunity comes to make a change in your life, you actually have to consider it.

For example, I've talked with many people about their health and fitness goals, and they'll ask me for advice. When the subject turns to nutrition, for instance, I suggest that they should increase their consumption of vegetables. Typically they answer, "Oh, I don't like vegetables. What else can I do?" That tells me they haven't opened their mind to the possibility of new things. And they probably don't even realize it. What they really want, possibly without knowing it, is for me to tell them the things they are already doing will give them the results they want. It's likely that that's not going to happen, of course, because they wouldn't have asked me what to do if they were already getting what they wanted.

The barriers to new ways must be lowered first. Their cup must be empty before anything new can be poured in. As you read you must, at least temporarily, embrace the option of changing something in your life. Stop thinking in terms of "*I don't,*" and start thinking "*I may ... .*" That word, "may," will open the door to opportunities in your life that you can't imagine.

Instead of imagining walls around you, imagine paths around you, leading away in different directions.

The mind game

Happiness is primarily a state of mind. I know external factors affect our state of being; however, I believe one of the problems facing people today as they strive for happiness, is placing too much emphasis on the external. I realize that having enough money is better than not having enough money, for example. External things come and go, but I don't want my happiness to come and go. So much of your life is just in your state of mind. If you broadened the possibilities in your mind, you broadened the possibilities in your life.

Do you want to leave worry behind? Changing your thoughts about life will have to occur first. "Oh, I'm just a worrier," you say. Then I hope worry makes you happy, because you haven't given your mind permission to see yourself as someone who doesn't worry about stuff. So the worrying will continue. You must give yourself permission to think any way about things that you haven't thought of them before.

What I want you to receive from this book is no matter your age, personality type, history, experiences, or what have you, the first step toward a life of everyday happiness and contentment is to *change* the pre-determined structure constructed in your mind. That structure is probably built with words, such as can't, don't, never, always, like, hate, should, won't.

As you begin actively deconstructing your mind, you will begin to realize the freedom to accept new ways of looking at situations of life. Things that you once automatically reacted to in a negative manner won't have quite the power they once had over you. Also, you will start becoming better able to find contentment and joy in things that you may have never before considered.

This is the launch pad for your new outlook, which will allow the other processes we will discuss to take place in your life so that you can live with a peace and contentment you may not have had.

Here is a little exercise you can do to help lower any barriers that may exist, known or unknown:

1) Choose a topic that typically polarizes people: a political or social topic, for example.
2) Sit quietly and imagine every opinion you could have about the subject—not every opinion you have, but every opinion you *could* have—considering all sides to the issue.
3) As you consider each point, try to empathize actively with each differing viewpoint.

This is not in any way an attempt to alter your ideals or values, but an opportunity to exercise your brain to be open to all things. It helps us limit an emotional response to thoughts that would normally provoke us toward one.

Picture a dear friend or valued loved one having a differing viewpoint to yours, and picture yourself, in spite of that difference, loving and cherishing them even more. This will help you broaden the scope of your thoughts about things, which will begin the process of you living happily, regardless of what's happening around you.

Chapter 2
Time

If you want a happy life you have to have a happy today.

When are you living? You read it correctly; not where, but *when* are you living?

In my opinion, this subject is a critical pivot point in a person being able to create newfound happiness and contentment in their life.

I believe too many of us today are living our lives for some other time than now.

We speak of time in states of past, present, and future. Our lives are made up of time. Time is life. If it weren't for time existing, passing and continuing on, there would be no living. The thing I believe people have missed about living is they look at time in their lives equally.

Stay with me here. While this may sound a little whacked out, I believe you can revolutionize your living by taking time to absorb these thoughts about time. Remember my advice in Chapter 1 about removing the barriers to your thinking? An hour of time is still an hour whether past, present, or future. This is why we believe it's all the same.

But it's not at all the same.

Time in the past existed or we wouldn't have memories and experiences. The past has value. This value, however, lies only within the framework of what we learned when that past was the present. If you burned your hand on a hot stove as a child, for example, you have probably carried that memory with you as you've matured. That memory aids you in the sense that you are more careful around hot objects because of the pain you remember from childhood.

There is value in memory of the past.

The future is time also. It's just time that hasn't come into being yet. It also has value. The beauty of the future is that you have power to alter it to fit your own desires. Anything can take place in the future. Not everything will, but it can. We can set goals for the future to be something or do something we're not being or doing right now. We can dream and then put into action the steps necessary to fulfill those dreams in the future. The future can be just about anything you desire it to be if you're willing to do what it takes to make that future a reality when it arrives.

The future has value also.

Why all this talk about the past and the future? I believe that many people today, who are searching for happiness and peace in their lives, are trying to live in either one or the other of those times; and possibly even both. You see, its' not that there's anything wrong with thinking about the past or the future, but living has to do with the present.

The gift of the present

My wife, Bobbi, and I were talking about this a few years ago, and I explained a revelation I had concerning time. I've seen so many people who were having problems with someone because of something that happened in the past. I wouldn't dream of minimizing someone's pain, but I can't imagine many of the horrible feelings some people carry around with them every day because of painful experiences in their past. Maybe you are carrying that pain inside right now. My prayer is that you begin, now, to get free of that thing and live joyfully.

Some of us are consumed with what is going to happen. We strain today with making sure that what we've planned for tomorrow will play out the way we imagined it would. So often we overload ourselves with the pressure of accomplishment and setting goals. We think that if our tomorrow isn't perfect, life will fall apart while imagining: *"What if I have a health crisis?" "What if I get laid off at work?" "What if I lose a loved one?"*

The good thing about the future is that anything can happen. The bad thing about the future is that anything can happen.

Jesus said, "Don't worry about your life. Who of you by working can add a single hour to his life?" (Mat. 6:25, 27) Planning is fine. Not being able to adapt to changes as the future unfolds is a peace stealer.

A wise man once said, yesterday is gone forever. It will never occur again in your life. Tomorrow is only a figment of your imagination, for when it gets here you will re-name it "today."

Today is where you live.

I told my wife one day, "If we're going to live a happy life we have to be happy on all the normal everydays." You see, today is *when* you're living; not yesterday, not tomorrow. If you want a happy life you have to have a happy today.

Life is primarily made up of all the regular days of life. The birthdays, vacations and holidays are a very small sliver of the time that comprises your life. You can't afford to wait for those times to be happy.

Wanting longingly for the good times of the past to return in order to be happy is a dead end street. Today is the time—each day of your life no matter how ordinary—that you must learn to be at peace. Tomorrow is a possibility, not a guarantee of happiness. Today is the only day that you can truly affect how you feel.

What time is it?

Everyone has the same amount of time. Our happiness, or the lack there of, can be dependent on how our time is spent, perceived and balanced. Let's break this down and look closer at time.

Perspective

The same amount of time can feel completely different based on our perception of it. For example, one minute staring at a beautiful woman is not the same as one minute holding your hand on a hot stove. Each is exactly one minute with a completely different perception of how it passes. We don't get to choose how much time we have, but we have power over the feel of its passing.

My wife's father once told her, "It's *your* time. *You* decide what to do with it." That decision will affect our happiness positively or negatively. My mindset will determine the quality of my time spent living. What you choose to look at determines what will grow inside of you.

Think about this question: When you're driving to work where is your mind? Are you thinking about deadlines at work? Wondering if you locked the door at home? Maybe you're thinking about a person you don't enjoy being around? Paying a bill? Traffic?

Why not take that time to extract all the joy and beauty you can from your commute? You have to be there anyway, and you're going to get to work anyway. Clear your mind of all other things, and look around. Consciously take your mind *off* of everything else, and give yourself permission to not think about any of the other things until you get to work. Notice the sky and the clouds. Focus on trees, people walking, or look for wildlife. Turn on your favorite music. Take that time to nurture yourself. Relax. Pray. Do something during that time for your inner self.

This is just one of those times in our day when things like this can be done. It's not so much what you're doing, but more about the state in which you're placing your mind. "Extracting the joy" is what I call it; finding the beauty that's there already. This may not sound like much to you now, but trust me, I believe that with practice, you will see a cumulative effect on your life. Remember, those minutes add up and will turn into hours in your life that you can begin experiencing a much happier outlook on life.

Make this your new plan for everything you do with your time: finding the beauty that's there. I know that there are things in life that aren't pleasant; I'm not trying to tell you that this is magic and that you can snap your fingers and never be disappointed. I am saying, however, that if you choose, you can start relieving your mind more and more. You can learn to find more pleasantness in places you have been overlooking in your routine.

<u>Balance</u>

Dividing our time into blocks of different activities is something that all too often happens *to* us instead of *by* us.

A great help to our well being is to properly divide our time daily. When we don't take this into our own hands we are setting ourselves up for frustration. This won't just happen. You must take the reins on this. Outside influences on our time are too many and too haphazard to leave it to chance.

Order brings comfort. Walk into a messy room where nothing is in its place, for example, and immediately agitation begins to set in. Conversely, walk into a room where things are arranged in an orderly fashion, and a soothing feeling begins to wash through your mind. Notice, I didn't say "clean" just "orderly." Clean is better than dirty, but the point is, all that has to happen is that things are in their place. When you begin to bring order into your time, comfort will often follow.

The book of Ecclesiastes states, "There is a time for everything, and a season for every activity under heaven." (3:1) Begin to make space for things within your daily routine that ensure balance between work and relaxation, between obligation and self-discovery, between exertion and relaxation, and between the physical and the spiritual.

Realize though, not every activity that can be done nee(be done every day. Some days require more work than other while other days require you to be with people most of the When you have a work–filled day it will be important to happiness to immediately prioritize some personal relax; time. As an introvert, when I have been around people a] have to have time by myself to pull away and build back my er reserves. Extroverts can hardly understand this. We will covei in a later chapter.

As you move through the ins and outs of your daily rou begin to actively focus on building balance into it. This will re(some focus for a while until it becomes nearly second na Actively take control of your routine, and ensure you are kee things balanced. This strikes at the core of a life of daily m and physical well being.

The key to happiness, remember, is in the daily routine in the far-off plans.

A note of caution: Balance works in all directions. We just play and rest all the time. Work is crucial to the equa Work can bring a satisfaction that rest cannot. Work re in accomplishment. Accomplishment brings about a sen wellbeing that nothing else can equal. Work doesn't always r earning money. Personal improvement, home improvemeni relational improvement also are categories of "work." They al their own kind of dividends. The idea is to keep in perspectiv balance of the daily, weekly and monthly schedule.

Joseph Cardillio, in his book "Be like Water," (2003) about Bruce Lee and his famous one-inch punch. Lee w demonstrate this for crowds. He would have a person star front of him while holding some phone books against their (Lee would hold his fist an inch from the phone books, his almost extended, and build his concentration. Then wit explosion of energy, from only one inch away, he would s the books, sending the participant reeling backward, somet

falling to the ground. When asked about the power of his punch, Lee would explain that it wasn't all about the continued forward thrust, but that it was crucial to retract the fist just after contact, pulling away. This left all the energy within the chest of the person being hit. Balance, therefore, was in striking and pulling away.

If there is actually a "time and a season for everything," then our lives should evidently include a variety of things to do. Time, if you balance your days, will balance itself during your week. If you balance your weeks, your months, in turn, will take care of themselves. This changes when you have an extended period of either work or relaxation.

During those periods, extra thought must also be given to the neglected activity. This can be phased back into a schedule of balance again fairly quickly.

A component of living happily is to include variety. You may have to think about this a little more than you believe. Sometimes we get into such a rut in life that when we do have free time for fun, we fall back into the most familiar activities. Why? Because it's comfortable to do so. We don' have to work at it. At times this comfort is what we need. There are times, though, that variety is more in order. Try new things. This will add a dimension to your reality that was missing before. Once you become accustomed to injecting variety, then a new sense of freedom and exploration will be added to your life, bringing greater satisfaction and fullness.

Who's the boss?

When it comes to spending your time, always remember: you're the boss.

You get to decide how your time is spent. You might say, "My boss says I have to be at work at 8 o'clock, and I don't get off until 5 o'clock." But who agreed to that? You did. If you don't want to do that, start looking for another job with different hours. I'm not trying to be demeaning with this analogy. This is part of you opening your mind to *all* the possibilities of how your time is

spent. The best decision for now may very well be to stay in that job until you find one you want more. But you're at least entertaining the question in your mind.

Regardless of your circumstances, though, you are in charge. True contentment in life will elude you if you see your time as being controlled by external forces. It's not necessarily easy, but you must become the one who decides what happens with your time. As you gradually get used to taking control, it will become easier.

Remember, saying "no" is a perfectly legitimate answer to a question. Some people struggle with this and usually find themselves greatly frustrated. Saying "no" doesn't mean you're a bad person, it means you have options. It means the word is *part* of your vocabulary. Don't say "No" all the time, however. Remember balance. When someone asks you to do something for them, and you know you're flooded with obligations, you owe it to yourself, and them, to say "no."

We all get 24 hours a day. Start taking authority over all that will occur within your 24. As you become more accustomed to balancing your time, adjusting the variety of it, and living in the present, you will see peace begin to flow. A greater calm will be the rule of your time instead of the exception.

Chapter 3
Fear

Fear may be the ultimate enemy to happiness. It stops us in our tracks. It ruins otherwise good times. Fear is a hidden, unseen attacker. Fear has to be controlled or it will run rampant in our lives, out of control, and creating havoc.

The late president Franklin D. Roosevelt, 32nd President of the United States, said in his first inauguration speech in 1933, "The only thing we have to fear is fear itself." We should be afraid of being afraid, and take steps in our lives to minimize it, ignore it, and control it.

Some fear is appropriate. If a raging maniac is breaking into your home you should experience some fear. In that case, it will drive you into action; however, it still must be controlled. Fear left unchecked becomes panic. A person panicking is out of control, unable to use their faculties properly. They become a defenseless victim to whatever is threatening them.

As a professional firefighter, I experienced the leading edge of panic once in a structure fire. A fellow firefighter and I were well into a house when fire erupted behind us, between our position and the door we entered. With fire ahead and growing behind us, my alarm on my breathing apparatus sounded, signaling my air was running out. I was quickly passing through fear and entering panic. We made it out in the nick of time, fortunately; and, as I said, some fear is appropriate and even healthy.

Much of the fear we experience throughout our lives is unwarranted. The key is to properly assess threatening fears, categorize them as warranted or unwarranted (and to what degree), and quickly deal with them. Not seizing control as early as possible gives fear time to take hold in our minds.

Fear is a fast–moving predator. It will race through your mind, growing like a wildfire, consuming all of the rational thought in its way. Out–of–control fear will paralyze you. In the martial arts we discuss and train for threatening situations with physical violence. Without training, when confronted with violence, many people freeze completely. If they do act, it will be with gross motor movements that cannot control the situation because of the adrenaline dump into their blood stream caused by irrational fear. That's why we train, to gain control over it.

The same thing applies to the everyday fears we encounter. We can train ourselves to gain control over them. We may not win every time, but the more we train the better we get. The better we get, the more we are able to control and overcome fear.

Common fears

Let's look at a few of the more common fears people experience; see if you recognize any of these from your own life:

Fear of other peoples' opinion of you

Until they break free, most people won't admit to fearing what other people think about them. This is a common fear. I couldn't count how many times I've seen grown men fall apart because they were told that another person they know said something derogatory about them. Some people are ashamed that this bothers them. They probably don't logically reason all this out in their head.

All they can say to themselves over and over is "I can't believe they said that about me!" Upon further discussion with someone who's experiencing this, eventually I get around to encouraging them to not let it bother them. Instantly and almost without exception, they snap back defensively "Oh, I'm not!" It's almost an ingrained physical reaction. At that point, it is blatantly obvious than it *does* bother them. Adding insult to injury, what was supposedly said about them may not even have been said. If it was said, it may not even be true. But if it is true, it may not have been told accurately. How can you get to the bottom of it? You can't.

I was bothered by this myself, until I heard Dr. Murdock say on a television program something that changed my life forever. He said when you hear that someone you know has slandered you or told something to smear you, don't get upset. Don't react to it. This is just the *one* you've heard about—there may be 50 more complaints you know nothing about. You can't even deal with all of those because you don't even know who they are. So remember, when you hear something like this the next time, this is only the one you have heard about.

If you embrace the idea that people may be talking about you—right or wrong—and that there's nothing you can do about it, it will free you to let go and live in peace when you do find out. Accept this idea. Embrace it. You will be set free from the opinions of others.

Fear of the unknown

Often times we are afraid of doing something because we don't know what the results will be. It seems strange to stop and think about this and what it entails. You might be unsatisfied with your life currently but won't take steps to make changes because of what you might have to do. Well, if you're unsatisfied with the status quo, why not do something, anything, to change it? Happiness doesn't come from being unsatisfied with life and just staying in that same situation day after day. If your today is unacceptable, but your tomorrow is going to be exactly like it, then your tomorrow is going to be unacceptable, too.

The unknown, if left unchecked in our minds, will destroy our daily peace. The unknown will create horrible imaginations in your mind if you don't take precautions to ensure that it won't. What we fail to realize is that the unknown can be good and bad.

Why do we often buy into the belief that if we try something new it probably isn't going to work anyway? This is one of those areas in our mind we need to open to change. Don't give fear of the unknown any power over you. Take charge yourself. Tell yourself, I will *not* fear what might or might not occur. I can be happy as well as not! Start telling yourself that you get to decide. Reject thoughts of failure.

I have found in my life that most of the things I feared might happen, never happen. Because your mind has such creative ability, it will dream up all sorts of horrible outcomes of almost anything we attempt. Then what you end up doing is dwelling on all those dark possibilities.

For example, you notice a dark spot on your skin and show it to a friend, who tells you to have it checked out. Negative thoughts have already begun. You visit the doctor, who looks at it and tells you it's "a little suspicious." You set an appointment to have it biopsied and removed, and go home. By this time you're having a hard time *not* thinking about the horrors of cancer. You're Googling photos of melanoma and reading about treatments.

The day comes, and it's removed. The doctor says he'll call you with the results. You're now a zombie. You've read everything you can get your hands on by now. Close friends have re-assured you, but to no avail.

The call comes. It's benign. No problem. You breathe deeply and relax. The very thing that consumed you for days never occurred.

Many times we fear something that's not going to happen. If it does happen, there will be time to concern ourselves with it then.

Fear of rejection

Another area of unwarranted fear is rejection. To most people, the thought of someone rejecting them is devastating; it could be in friendship, love, work or what have you. Can you remember a time when you weren't chosen until last for a team in a physical education class? It's a nasty feeling. We really didn't know at the time how to properly deal with that sort of emotion. As we mature, however, we can learn.

There are two ways to learn: mistakes and mentors.

You may have heard people say, *"They've got to learn the way I did—the hard way."* This is simply not true. If we learned only by experience there would never be any progress. We would repeat the same mistakes generation after generation. Unfortunately, many people do this. I just don't want to be like the masses that keep having the same problems repeatedly.

A better way is to find someone who has learned a lesson and learn from them by reading a book about their experiences, for instance, and then putting into practice what that person taught you through the pages of that book.

I remember hearing a story about this by a businessman. He was at a seminar on successful people, and at the break, he told his aide to buy one of everything the speaker had at his table. The young aide came back without anything. When asked why he came back empty handed, the aide replied, "That's going to cost $1,200!" The businessman said, "Son, go back and get all of it. It took him 70 years to learn what I will know in hours!"

Reading this book is putting you on the fast track toward throwing off fear and ushering in more peace and contentment; understanding that most of the time, we simply give ground to it. If we decide now that we're going to change and learn how to handle and minimize fear, and begin to implement those changes, we are on the move toward a life of greater joy and peace, unbroken by the destructiveness of fear.

Chapter 4
Relationships

*"Always keep your words soft and sweet because
someday you may have to eat them."*
— *My grandfather Lawrence "Pap" Haverly*

There is potential when two humans interact with one another—potential for great, comforting interaction and fellowship. On the other hand, world wars have been fought because of interaction between people.

The potential is endless. For the sake of this chapter, I'm going to assume you prefer peace and love and warmth in your relationships. If not, you need the help of a professional.

Why is it that no matter how hard we try to build positive relationships some eventually derail? I believe the reasons are numerous and varied. We will look into the dynamics of relationships and discuss some of the variables. In doing so, you will begin to see some of them in your own relationships. Not all relationships have the same needs. What are the needs in one relationship from another? I will suggest ways to make them better and more fulfilling.

Just as important, and I believe overlooked, is what you *can't* do to make your relationships better. It's important to your happiness to understand the differences. And finally, I'll suggest how you can guard your own well being in relationships. As you might discover, this may be the most important aspect of all.

There are many principles influencing our relationships, but let's explore three that I believe will help you create joy and happiness in your life and within your relationships:

Principle 1: Doing your part

When you have a relationship with someone (whether romantic, family, or friend), both parties need to apply themselves to make it a good experience for both. If both aren't contributing, it's only a matter of time before the relationship will erode.

My wife and I have helped people in their marriages through counseling and mentorship. We tell them that marriage is not a 50%-50% situation, it's a 100%-100% situation. Both parties must give all to it. If one is holding out to see if they get theirs, it won't work.

For example, what happens if you're in a friendship with someone, and you're doing your best, but they're not holding up their end? To keep your own happiness intact you have to overlook an insult or negligence in the relationship. You can't hold up their end. *They* have to do that.

The Apostle Paul wrote "In as much as it has to do with you, live in peace with all people." (Rom. 12:18) You can only do what *you* can do. When others won't, you have to release their part of it to them. You can't let yourself be responsible for all of that.

This is part of living happily. Sometimes unpleasant things happen with others. When they do, you must understand what you can do about it, and what you can't do about it. You must train yourself to let go of unwarranted guilt, which will rob you of all peace in your life.

This is not easy.

At first it can gnaw at you continually when a close friend deserts or distances themselves from you. After reflecting on it and deciding you've done all you can do, you must release yourself from any animosity they hold. You need to work at your relationships and be sensitive to other people's needs and feelings; however, you can't find fault with people who leave you over justifiable wrongs left unchecked.

Sometimes no matter what you do someone will find fault with you. That's when you have to understand that it's *their* problem. See it that way. Don't own what's not yours. This will bring serenity to your mind. You will begin to feel strength you didn't have before. It's empowering when you begin to realize that you are very much in control of your happiness. You're not completely dependent on another person emotionally.

The more you understand and practice this, the better you get at it. The better you get, the less discouraged or hurt your feel. In turn, that results in a more level emotional life, which will be more free and fulfilling.

Principle 2: There are two sides to a coin

When you have a relationship with someone it's critical to remember that people don't see things the same way. For example, you've probably heard how two people can witness a car wreck, but can differ in their account of what happened. Is someone lying? Often not. Both people *believe* what they saw is true, but how they experienced the moment dictates a different scene in their minds.

To enjoy our relationships, we must learn to leave room for differences. It's disturbing to me to see two people who like each other in almost every way, for one to find out the other holds opposing political viewpoints, for instance. Suddenly everything changes, and the warmness and comfort of the relationship is drowned by one difference between them. I'm not always right, and it has helped me develop empathy toward others to keep this realization in the forefront of my mind.

To live with a calming comfort in our relationships, we must leave room for differences and encourage dissent by adopting that mindset before it happens. Living prepared for conflict makes it so much easier to handle than waiting to try to handle it when it occurs.

I have found that my life is more full and balanced when I allow others into my life who may not see things the way I do. I want to be respected for my personal viewpoints. How, then, can I not be respectful of others' viewpoints when they stand opposed to mine? The only way my wife and I have been married 35 years is that we have learned to allow for the differences that make us individuals and embrace those differences within our marriage. You are not going to change them; you must learn to love *with* differences. This is at the center of respect.

<u>Principle 3: Forgiveness</u>

I think many people have this one backward in their mind. We have a tendency to view forgiveness as something that benefits the one who has offended another. To be sure, it is a blessing to be forgiven for something we've done. We all need it eventually, and when forgiveness comes, it's like a refreshing shower flowing over our spirit. The overlooked part is when we are the offended party. Too often we don't realize the importance of forgiving someone who has offended us. It is not just for their benefit, but also for ours.

Happiness of being will slip from your grasp as long as you harbor unforgiveness in your heart. This may seem unnatural or abnormal, but it is a huge key that will unlock doors to freedom and peace within. To forgive, especially when it's not necessary, is a powerful tool at your disposal that will aid in your quest for living life with contentment and peace.

No forgiveness, no peace. Know forgiveness, know peace.

Your ego will struggle with this. You will hear yourself

saying "They don't deserve forgiveness!" Maybe they don't. Don't you believe you deserve to live unencumbered by the weight of unforgiveness you would have to carry around each day? Do it for *you*! Don't punish yourself by hanging on to something someone *else* has done. Remember the reality of it. You didn't do it. They did. Don't carry a load that's not yours to carry. Never empower another person to place upon you something that was their fault. That's what happens when we don't forgive. We willingly keep ourselves shackled to a negative situation. Let go. Let that situation out of your life and create the space for refreshing and release to come in and live there.

Casting the first stone

It's so easy to look at another and find every fault they have. I would like to tell you this isn't true or that most people don't do that; but they do. *We* do. It's not easy to admit, but if you chose to acknowledge that, you will have helped yourself.

Have you ever found yourself describing something that is a fault in someone else's life only to have someone present say "well, I've heard you say that, too," or "I saw you do the same thing"? It's a humbling experience, believe me.

The trouble is, even if you haven't actually heard it, someone around you has probably said it about you or thought it when they heard you talking about someone else. Finding fault with others will create unpleasantness in our own lives, sooner or later. Jesus pointed out his problem when a woman was dragged to him by the so called "religious people." They accused her of being caught in the act of doing something awful. They were emphatic that she should be stoned to death, and they wanted Jesus to approve. Instead, Jesus paid them almost no attention. He finally answered, "Let any one of you who is without sin be the first to throw a stone at her." (John 8:7) One by one, they walked away knowing that their sin simply had not been made public. When no one was left but her, Jesus told her to go home, but to leave her life of sin.

Jesus' lesson is one we can take to heart to keep ourselves from becoming entangled in criticism and controversy. None of us is perfect. If you're like me, you're far from it.

We shouldn't be quick to jump on the band wagon in bashing a co-worker or acquaintance, for example, because we know down deep we've done wrong, too. Oh, we'll usually justify it in our minds thinking "well I've never done *that* before, maybe other stuff, but never *that!*" Or, "I would never say something like *that!* I'm no saint, but not that." You're right, you're no saint. Neither am I. When we point at others, we're no better than them.

Try this next time: When someone does something obviously wrong, overlook it. Yes, overlook it. I know I don't want someone pointing out what I may do wrong. Why do it to others? It won't do you or me any good. It can only bring bitterness into our lives. There is a peace and level of satisfaction that will come when you show a person mercy, especially when you know they are guilty.

Overlooking an offense is an act of graciousness. Giving grace will bring graciousness. Let someone else be a fault finder. Unless it's part of your job, or you're turning in a criminal, let someone else play that role. Even then you can't do it if you have to, without bitterness or personal vindictiveness. I know, very well, there have been times I would love to have been shown mercy for some things. Being someone who gives relief to the soul who is in trouble is refreshment to your own soul.

I read a note I found after my grandfather Lawrence Haverly's death. On it he had written "Always keep your words soft and sweet because someday you may have to eat them." Well said, Pap.

Chapter 5
Health

"The journey of a thousand miles begins with a single step." — *Lao Tzu*

There is so much to say here about creating better health in relationship to living a happy, fulfilling life that I'm almost giddy just thinking about it. I have been deeply involved with health and fitness most of my life. As a result, I know firsthand the benefits good health and fitness can have in all areas of life. Please be patient and stay with me if you haven't been a fitness type. I won't attempt to turn you into some fitness junky, unless you want to be.

If you haven't been a health enthusiast you simply cannot know how much this affects your mental outlook on life. So that's why I ask you to stay with me. But it's totally OK to have never delved into this area. I just want you to be aware of everything in life that can add to your happiness of living. That's why you're reading this book. This is an area that can significantly add satisfaction to everyday life.

Quality of Life

In my opinion, one of the most important factors to ongoing happiness is having a high quality of life; specifically the mental and physical aspects of life.

Being well supplied financially also can be referred to as "quality of life." We will touch on this later. Right now, quality is in the context of how well you are doing physically and mentally and, more importantly, how those two factors affect each other.

I don't believe we can overstate the effect good health can have on the mental or psychological well being of a person. We have a saying in martial arts: "Where the head goes, the body follows." This is meant physically; however, wherever you go mentally, your body also will follow. If your body gets in better condition, you mind will follow by getting in better condition. There is probably no one greater thing you can do for your mental outlook than improving your health.

Well, how do we go about this? You can't just say "be healthier" and make it happen. Although speaking positive things about your health will actually help in the process. How do we actually go about this? There are two concepts I would like you to understand first:

1) It's easier than you might think to make great improvements to your health; and
2) You should adopt any changes as a lifestyle, not something you do once and expect lifelong results.

Let's break it into more bite-size pieces: Health and its two pillars—exercise and nutrition.

The 'Kingdom' of Health

The iconic late fitness guru and television personality, Jack LaLanne said, "Exercise is king and nutrition is queen. You put them together, and you have a kingdom." Nothing could be more true. The kingdom of your health is built on these two pillars. Exercise is probably the one thing you can do that will bring the most satisfaction into your life. Whether rich or poor, there's no substitute for feeling stronger and healthier. When you decide to raise the level of your health your quality of life is higher. When the quality of your life is high, you feel better about everything, and live life much happier.

Pillar 1: Exercise

The foundation of your health level is built upon the presence or absence of regular exercise in your normal routine. If you don't exercise regularly, start now. "The journey of a thousand miles begins with a single step." (Lao Tzu)

This is not a "how to" book on fitness; however, there are some critical thoughts on exercise I want to address. I have lived a life of exercise and still do at 53 years of age. I've seen the barriers that stop people and found things you can use to help you in your journey toward good health.

People have asked me what exercise routine they should do, and I say, "The one that you will *do!*" Let it sink in for a minute. The best plan in the world is useless if you don't actually do it. If you're going to end up quitting, it's no good for you. Find what you will keep up and do that.

A friend may do triathlons, and you may admire how diligently they train, but if you can't or won't put that kind of time into training, find something else you will dedicate yourself to doing. Whatever you choose, start slowly. Don't start walking five miles a day on the first day. You may feel like you can do it easily. But don't do it. You have plenty of time to build up. Your body has to have time to adapt to new stresses on it. Overdoing it taxes your recuperation more than you will realize.

Listen. You don't have to get a gym membership. You don't have to use exercise machines or devices. You don't have to find a personal trainer. You don't even need to spend money. You have your body, and you have gravity. That's all you need. Society has been so brainwashed into believing we need gimmicks and gadgets that we can't understand how to exercise without them.

What am I recommending? I recommend walking, jogging, running, climbing small hills, climbing big hills, swimming, calisthenics, sit-ups, leg raises, squats, lunges, push-ups, stairs, and so on. If you need to, find a book on bodyweight training and choose what fits you. Bicycling is great. If you love the gym, that's fine. I'm just saying you don't need it.

When choosing exercise movements choose those that use large portions of your body or compound movements as opposed to just one small part at a time, isolating one muscle or body part. This is more time economical and, most importantly, more functional training for use in real life activities.

For example, for lower body training, instead of using a leg extension machine, just do bodyweight squats. The latter works all the muscles of your lower body, not to mention it aids in balance and agility, which is more closely related to normal life functions.

I recommend you do exercise with two different goals in mind and divide them into these categories: Strength and endurance.

1) Strength exercise is more important than most people think. This would mean moving your body against resistance for short duration. For a beginner just leaning against a wall with your hands and pushing away would work for upper body strength conditioning.

2) Endurance exercise involves using the whole body as a unit, and moving it in a way that can be sustained for time, which taxes the cardiopulmonary system more. A beginner's example might be a one mile walk.

Combining both of these aspects into your program ensures a well rounded affect on the body. Don't be fooled. You need both. How will all this new movement help me live happier, you ask? Well, one immediate benefit you get from fairly vigorous exercise is the chemicals released into your bloodstream called endorphins.

These chemicals cause a great sense of well being in your brain. Years ago it was referred to as a "Runner's high." You don't have to run to get it. It comes with vigorous exercise of any kind. I have noted times of stress in my life when nothing more than a 30 minute workout changed my entire outlook for the day. There is a sense of accomplishment and satisfaction that comes over you and lasts a long time when these endorphins are released into your system.

Something else begins happening when you exercise regularly. You start looking better. Please understand, I don't recommend you do it primarily for that reason. I'd rather think of it as a great side effect. People have differing results in how their looks change depending on what they're doing, their age, body type, and genetic makeup. But chances are, you will see a marked difference in your appearance. When you look better, you feel better. When you feel better you live happier.

The reason I focus on functional training is that it will help your body be able to do the things in life that you have to do and the things you want to do. Keeping up with your children is easier, climbing the steps is easier, and recreation with others is easier. When limitations begin falling away, enjoyment begins to rise. The more you can do, the more you want to do. This begins to open the possibilities of life, giving you more options, and bringing greater satisfaction of living.

For those of us who aren't spring chickens anymore, functional training keeps us able to perform daily activities without hindrance into our later years. In plain English: It keeps you younger.

If you are already advanced in years, you may be surprised at how much you can turn back the hands of time. Remember, you don't know what you don't know. You have no idea how agile you may become. People have made amazing gains doing only a limited amount of exercise, especially when it's geared toward functionality.

Agility, balance, and endurance are physical components that heighten when exercise is regular. Being able to do things you only did when you were younger, and being able to do them longer, come from moderate exercise. I recommend exercising at least three times per week, and no more than six. Try to split your training between strength and cardiovascular. If you have to choose, I recommend you opt for more strength training. Just don't forsake the cardio.

I have barely scratched the surface on all there is to say about exercise. However, it is enough to give you the foundation to get you going. Remember, when you train your body, you get results:

- you feel better,
- you perform better,
- you look better,
- you will physically be better than before.

All of this lifts your spirit, raises self-esteem, and builds confidence, which leads to a much higher level of satisfaction with life, and a steady sense of well being.

Pillar 2: Nutrition

Remember, she's the "Queen" of this kingdom. Again, this is a subject that requires a book of its own. What I want to do for you is to condense it into a few concepts instead of quoting statistics and having you memorize chemical compounds.

Following are some nutritional ideas for you to consider and how you might benefit from them:

1) **Eat more often, but less each time.**

Have a *minimum* of three meals a day—including *always* eating breakfast. If you decide to make it four or five meals, you should not eat very much more in total for the day. Each meal should be in smaller amounts, but more frequent. This will provide a level stream of nutrients to the body throughout the day.

2) **Eat a variety of foods daily.**

Don't fight this. Learn to do it. You *need* vegetables. You need some fruit. You need protein like eggs, dairy, meat, and fish. Eat some nuts, not just peanuts, but tree nuts. Learn the habit of sneaking veggies into dishes if you don't care for them otherwise. Focus as much as you can on eating green foods. Here again, I'm not giving you a college credit on nutrition. Explore these concepts in more depth on your own.

3) **Cut down on carbohydrates.**
   - You don't have to cut carbs completely, just lower the amount. Find out the carb content of things you normally eat.
   - All foods are comprised of some ratio of four macro-nutrients: Protein, carbohydrates, fat, and water.
   - Most people eat way too many carbohydrates. Many high carb foods are healthy; however, we overdo it, badly. High carb intake raises your insulin level. That, in turn, causes your body to try to store body fat more than normal.
   - Lowering carbohydrate amounts will help you stay lean while eating a good amount of food.

4) **Corn and rice are not vegetables.**
   - They are grains. Grains are primarily a carbohydrate.
   - Pasta is made from wheat (a grain), and is high in carbs.

5) **Meat is good for you.**
   - Meat—not processed meat products like hot dogs, lunchmeats, and processed nuggets—is primarily

protein. It keeps muscle and connective tissues repaired, strong, and functional.

- Keep your protein intake frequent.

6) **Lower the amount of breaded and fried food you eat.**
   - Breading adds carbs then soaks up the oil it's fried in, adding calories and fat. Oil of all kinds is 100 percent fat. Fat has more than twice as many calories as either protein or carbohydrate.
   - Good fats come from olive oil, fish, and nuts; but even these are fats, and the calories per gram are still much higher than protein or carbohydrate. Go easy on them.

7) **Drink water.**
   - Water has zero calories. You need water, and you need more of it than you're probably getting now.
   - Reduce soft drinks drastically or quit.
   - Water makes every process in your body work. Drink more of it.

Weight loss

Good health should be a primary concern. However, if weight loss is high on your priority list, here are a few principles to keep in your regimen of greater health:

1) **Focus on *fat* loss, not weight loss.**

Personally, I never use scales. I really don't care what I weigh. Using a mirror and objectively judging what you see will tell you more than the scales will. Muscle and all other tissues weigh more than fat per unit of area. Many people solidify their muscle structure upon beginning exercise and may lose a little fat. They hop gleefully onto the scales expecting something wonderful, only to be shot down finding they haven't lost any weight. Worst of all, they may have even gained a pound or two. *"Arrgghh!"* they exclaim, shoving the scales into the closet. Their chances of staying on their program just fell to half because of that letdown.

- Muscle outweighs fat.
- What you see in the mirror will be more accurate than what you see on the scales.

2) For fat loss, your nutritional program will help you more than your exercise program.

I didn't say you don't need to exercise. Exercise is superb for good health. But for fat loss you can affect the most change by what you eat or don't eat. To eliminate 1,000 calories from your body through exercise is pretty grueling and will take some time. It takes zero time, however, to *not* eat something.

For example, if you eat a jelly doughnut every morning at break time, and your weight is staying the same, just by *not* doing that you will reduce your calorie count for the week by 2000 (assuming the doughnut contains at least 400 calories—it probably has more). And that's only counting weekdays. You have also improved your health because all of those empty calories contain very little nutrition, and a ton of junk.

3) On the flipside, don't reduce your calories or food intake drastically to lose weight.

All of that food is where you get all of your energy for exercise and moving around, as well as for the processes that go on internally to create the great health you're trying to attain. Take a moderate approach to all aspects of your health plan.

In conclusion, on the whole, people I know who put high levels of emphasis on their health appear to be the most level emotionally. They also appear to consistently maintain a good outlook on life. Even small gains will bring you more satisfaction than almost anything else you do. In growing healthier and fitter, you will grow happier and more satisfied with life. And the benefits of being healthier will also enable you to handle stresses of life with greater ease.

Chapter 6
Personality Types

Accept the way others around you
are, and the way you are.

To understand contentment with your life, you will first need to fully understand who you are. Many people think they know who they are just because they've lived with themselves their whole lives. To a point, that's true. However, many of us keep going about our lives never really trying to understand ourselves. We know what we feel, and we think that's all there is. Then in trying to find happiness, we focus on getting things we don't have. We also try to change the things outside us, assuming the internal is set in stone.

As you've hopefully realized by now, the key to true and lasting peace in life is finding it *in* life, not changing life merely thinking it will come. Sure, better jobs, more disposable income, and more free time help with some of life's problems. However, money is not the answer to every issue of life. I'm not trying to patronize you by saying these things don't matter, but even rich people deal with depression, and some beautiful people think they are ugly, and it's all they can think about.

A very wealthy famous person was asked: "How much money does it take to make you happy?" He replied, "Just a little bit more."

If we can learn things about ourselves and discover why these things work the way they do, we can begin unlocking even more areas of our life where we can lose the stress and build the joy. Also, we may learn things about those close to us with whom we live or whom we are near on a daily basis. This may allow us to co-exist with greater ease, making life more pleasant and fulfilling. With this in mind, let's explore some areas that I believe have potential to cause unnecessary friction. As you read through this next section, you may identify other areas of your nature where these principles apply and help in other aspects of your life.

Extravert vs. Introvert

When it comes to our personalities, most of us fall on either side of a line separating extraverts from introverts. What are they? Briefly, extraverts are considered outgoing, talkative, and gregarious. They love socializing with many, various people and, in general, like being with people. Introverts, on the other hand, enjoy being alone or prefer socially small numbers or just a close friend. They are more reserved, quite, and solitary.

"How is this important to my personal happiness?" you ask. When you understand yourself better you are more aware of your own needs and desires, and more specifically, why you have those particular needs. When dealing with others, you can better understand their personality types as well, what they will need and want, and what they like and why, thus allowing for better relations between you and others. Also, knowing what they can't tolerate and why helps you meet their needs, bringing peace and fluidity to the relationship. Additionally, you will be more equipped to explain why the things you need are so important. This is never more important than within a marriage relationship.

It's crucial to understand that the characteristics of an introvert, for example, aren't the ones they've chosen, they're the ones they innately have within them. You don't choose to be an extravert either. You are that way naturally. If you're an introvert you can't just become an extravert because your spouse wants you to be one.

Many people want to find fault with someone close to them because they don't share the same outlook on life and think they should simply change. They can't. They're born with these traits. For example, it can be frustrating for an extravert wife to understand why her introvert husband doesn't want to attend larger social functions, or vice versa. Many times in these situations this will create tension between the two. The tension stems from believing that their actions or wishes are their *choice*. They aren't a choice. This is who they are. This is how they were made. It's like trying to make a cat into a dog.

Peace and smoothness in relationship comes when understanding of the other turns to compassion for their feelings and needs. My wife Bobbi is an extravert. I am an introvert. Our marriage has greatly improved as a result of *embracing* the understanding of each other's personalities. As an extravert, she needs to periodically be with people. This gives her energy and enthusiasm. I don't particularly like those situations, but I want her to be happy so I go along. Not wanting me to be uncomfortable all the time, Bobbi limits those times now and then for my sake. She leaves those events full of energy and talking nonstop. I, on the other hand, gain my energy by seeking quite solitude. I expend energy in social settings and recharge by pulling back to alone time. She gains energy in social activities and slowly loses energy by not being with people for a while.

As you begin to see your own needs and the needs of others, your interactions with others is smoother and more satisfying. The key is to recognize and accept these traits in yourself, and in those around you. Often, misunderstandings occur when an extravert perceives an introvert as shy, backward, and socially inept; therefore viewing the introvert as personally flawed.

Nothing could be less true. Or an introvert may believe an extravert is chatty, scatterbrained and unable to be quiet or still for very long, or unable to think deeply. Again, the extravert is behaving opposite of how an introvert would, so it's hard for the introvert to be empathetic.

Being either way is neither good nor bad. It simply is. Accept the way others around you are and the way you are. Learn about it so it's easier to live and interact with each other.

Leaders and Followers

It is in some people's nature to lead. They surge to the forefront of any group quickly. Most of the time this is viewed as a positive quality, and it is, provided there is no leadership in place. When two leaders find themselves in the same group, one of them must give way graciously to the other, otherwise there will be a battle, of sorts, in personality or otherwise for sole leadership.

Leadership is necessary in life, but it's obvious that not everyone can be the leader. When good leadership already exists, a person with leadership qualities can be of value if they remain humble and watch for openings where additional leadership is requested by the primary leader. This can be extremely difficult for strong leaders to handle. Their ego may resist submitting to another, believing that they are the greater leader. They may very well be better, but unless they've been given the role of leader, they should defer to the authority in place to keep peace and promote unity and civility.

This is especially common in the workplace, particularly among men. For example, I've seen guys come unglued when the boss or supervisor asked man "A" to do a particular job that he knew that man could do, not knowing man "B" standing nearby was an expert in the matter. Sometimes man "B," cannot control his ego, or will not control it, or may never have thought about controlling it, in such a situation. Times like this are unpleasant. However, if we natural leaders are in such situations, we can avoid untold grief and stress by learning to slay our ego. Learning to submit to another whether you think you should or not, brings about a quiet, peaceful strength within.

The Proverbs state, "A fool shows his annoyance at once ... ." (12:16) Training ourselves to keep ego under control will not be easy, but will give you power you never knew existed. This includes power over anxiety and stress, and power to accept situations as they are, gliding over them as a reflection glides over the water, yet leaves the water undisturbed.

In today's society, especially in the United States of America, strong leaders are admired, almost idolized. But not everyone can lead. In every structured organization, there have to be followers or doers of the plan brought about by the leaders. Not only that, but there have to be more followers than leaders. Someone has to do the work. And the work needs to be done well. Clearly, following is misunderstood. If you are a natural follower, you are as essential as anyone in the world. I have found following, without causing strife for the leadership, is a quality that is quickly disappearing. There is a deep satisfaction in carrying out the orders of leadership with excellence that can't quite be equaled. Being a good follower is a highly noble endeavor. Many people's egos can't take following without question or disruption, however. We're taught today to question, protest, and speak up any time we disagree. There are times and places for such things, but not in every circumstance or venue.

Being a happy follower is good for leaders and good for the person following. If you are a natural follower don't let society pressure you into trying to transform yourself into a leader. It's true that sometimes a person is a potential leader but one who may need a self-esteem boost in order to discover his leadership qualities. A good follower who knows themselves should rest assured in understanding they are fulfilling their purpose. Don't let people tell you who you are or should be. When people try to mold you without your consent, you can avoid that energy they're putting in your way by flowing around it as water in a stream flows around a rock. You know yourself better than anyone. Live your life the way you decide, letting other opinions gently slide by you as you move with the flow of your life.

The Analyst vs. Free Spirit

An analyst is one who collects information, examines it, and categorizes the results so that they're useful in decision making. This is methodical and logical and, for many, as normal as brushing their teeth. Living life thinking through every decision, planning every day out carefully is completely normal, but to others, this kind of life is much too confining. These free spirits would rather plan as little as possible and take each day as it comes, which seems absolutely normal to them. Planning and strategizing life would be like prison to the free spirit.

You may be wondering why I have included a section concerning these two personality traits. Well, for a couple of reasons: I have a little bit of both in me, therefore I have thoughts on both for people who want more happiness in their lives. Additionally, I have observed others, who exhibit traits of either extreme. I've noticed they usually have some difficulty, wishing they could be a little more like the other one. I am a great proponent of you being who you are, accepting yourself and embracing your differences from others. However, sometimes we need to distinguish between something that is simply a unique difference to embrace, or a sticking point in our personal development that holds us back from achieving what we want.

No one is going to make you happy. You have to see to it yourself. Do you over analyze life, wising you could lighten up a little? Or, are you so free and loose in your lifestyle that you can't seem to accomplish things, or miss deadlines? Either end of the spectrum can be problematic. Remember, there is a proper balance to all aspects of life.

Bruce Lee said, "If you think too much about a thing, you'll never get it done." This is known as the "Paralysis of analysis." (Lee, 1975) The over analyzer has trouble moving from the analyzing phase to the decision making phase, and finally to the action phase. It's extremely frustrating when you can't quit thinking about something and simply make a decision. This person believes that further and further pondering will finally flip the light switch on, and the decision will materialize. Generally that's not what happens, however. Frustration will build bringing about more doubt and prolonging a decision or action. Usually you know when you've looked a problem over enough. That's the time to cease all further prolonging and act. The more this is done the less anxiety there will be the next time a decision must be reached. Try giving yourself an arbitrary deadline. If you haven't acted by then a choice *will* be made, good or bad. Stress from over analyzing will start to disappear, knowing it will be over by that time.

The free spirit is not encumbered by such issues. They'll live with it no matter what happens. They don't stress over having to come to a conclusion. Really, they have it a little better than the over analyzer. Stress is not really in their vocabulary. Being so carefree is great, but sometimes not ever being under stress can lead to never accomplishing your goals.

Scientifically, a response only results from stimulus. We must be stimulated to move. The knowledge of resulting consequences from missing a deadline is usually sufficient stimulus to cause us to respond by acting to accomplish it. When we're so freewheeling that we pay no attention to the demands of life we can cause ourselves undo heartache. The free spirit has to learn to *create* structure where often none exists, to avoid problems and issues in dealing with others in a world that strives to force too much structure upon them. We can learn to still live free and out-of-the-box, but allow enough structure to deal with others who haven't learned these lessons yet.

Obviously the moral of this story is the word "balance." You may lean one way or the other, but you can still balance yourself. It's when we tip over too far in any direction that we fall down. Learning to balance our lives, our ideas, our temperaments, our time, and every aspect of our lives, will create more peace, more contentment, and more enjoyment of everyday life.

Chapter 7
Recreation

Work equals productivity. Play equals creativity.

Recreation is very important to our sanity. For many of us, we won't need any prompting to realize we need to make time for enjoyment and relaxation. I think about it all the time. There are those, though, who just can't or won't cut out time in their lives for fun and enjoyment. People who are driven and highly goal oriented may not want to stop work long enough to have time for recreation.

There is an old time-tested saying: "All work and no play make Jack a dull boy." We need play to get our juices flowing. When we always focus on getting things done, we never get done the things that need to happen inside us. Rest and relaxation will produce fruit that labor never can. It's like trying to harvest apples from peach trees or walnuts from pecan trees. Work equals productivity. Play equals creativity.

Why is recreation so important? Because it actually "re-creates" us. When the crowds had been with them so long and his disciples were overworked, paraphrasing Jesus, he told his disciples to come away to a quiet place. (Mark 6:31) He knew the importance to them that they get away and relax. You can't work a machine constantly without shutting it off and doing maintenance now and then. If you want regular happiness within your life, then regular rest and recreation must become part of your life. What exactly does that look like? Well, it's a little different for everyone. Some people love adrenaline pumping activities like bungee jumping or racing motorcycles. For others, its reading, shopping, or going to the movies. My advice is to dabble in a range of activities from mild to wild.

What to do?

"Variety is the spice of life." (Cowper, 1785) To me, doing the same thing all the time for fun is too monotonous. I like to get outside and move. I also enjoy alone time, reading or watching a movie. Both types of activities are important, but in different ways. It seems that the quiet times of rest and tranquility are good for putting things *into* me. When I'm still and relaxed I can re-charge and build my reserves. Quiet, restful relaxation seems to allow us to soak healing and restoration into our body and mind. On the other hand, active physical activities seem to help in getting stuff *out* of me. For example, hiking and outdoor-related activities have a great way of purging our minds of stress and mental and physical tension. Fresh air, nature, movement, and companionship all press out of our lives the poison of pressure and stagnation we build up between times of recreation. When we get the bad out we have made room for the new good to come in.

Make an appointment

When do we do all of this? That's a good question. The answer is in your schedule. I can point you the way. You will have to see the answer. What I can tell you is this, You will have to schedule variety and recreation into your life. Chances are it won't just happen. For your own good and psychological well being, you must take control of your schedule and treat recreation like an appointment with another person. On several occasions, for instance, when asked if I could be somewhere at a certain time, I've replied "No. Sorry, I have an appointment at that time." I may have had a workout planned, a martial arts class, gone hunting, or planned rest scheduled. I don't offer reasons when asked. I just have an appointment. It might as well have been a doctor's appointment or a job interview. The fact is it's not anyone's business what your appointment is. Don't feel compelled to announce a reason that someone may punch holes in to coerce you to spending your time doing what *they* want you to do, rather than what *you* want to do. You must control your time; even your down time. Guard it preciously. If you don't, you will lose it. You should start seeing your recreation time as equally important to your life as your work time, time for others, sleeping time, and spiritual time. What you don't value will leave your life.

Level and Frequency

You must decide what makes you happy. What I like, you may not. I can tell you what I have found works for me, though, and you can keep what works for you and change what doesn't. The level and frequency of your recreation references the degree of its excitement and how often you engage in it. Generally speaking, I believe your goal should be to schedule frequent low level activities and less frequent high level activities. These may even be broken down further into very frequent low level and very infrequent high level activities.

Following are a few examples of these four categories of recreational activities:

1) **Very frequent low level:** Taking a bubble bath, reading a book, praying, meditating, enjoying a drink, sitting in a porch swing, and taking a walk.
2) **Frequent low level:** Date night with your spouse, playing golf, swimming, going to the movies, writing, and learning a sport.

3) **Infrequent high level:** Annual family vacation, deep sea fishing trip, weekend festival outings, and going to concerts.

4) **Very infrequent high level:** Hawaii vacation, trip to Europe, vacation home, and retirement.

I look forward to watching the evening news almost every night. I also look forward to heading out on vacation with my wife usually once or twice per year. But I look forward to both of them equally. I believe it's important to know you have a rest period ahead of you. Having something to look forward to is encouraging. It makes the toil of life much more bearable when you know there is fun and relaxation awaiting you.

As you read earlier, I'm not advocating simply living for the future. Just trying to get through the day only to try to enjoy a short period in the evening is ultimately unfulfilling by itself. You end up wishing most of your life away in hopes of a few minutes of joy. You must make all of your life as happy and enjoyable as possible.

When there is something ahead to look forward to, it brings more moments of excitement and anticipation into your every day moments. Sometimes the planning and the discussion of what you're going to do is almost as much fun as actually doing the activity. Bobbi and I have had a lot of fun getting excited over an upcoming outing. Having something planned can greatly enrich your everyday life, whether small or large, or both.

A final note on recreation: If you are a type "A" personality this may be more of a task for you than for others. Specifically, if you are the type who works when you are bored, you may have to modify your approach to the recommendations of this chapter. Honestly ask yourself if work a compulsion or a relaxation? I encourage you to truthfully examine yourself to determine whether you really *enjoy* working, or decide if it is an exercise in keeping you from other people, places or things that might want your attention. Once you are brutally honest with yourself about this, and you conclude that work *really* is your relaxation and rest, then by all means, do what makes you happy. Just remember, if you have loved ones who do not feel this way, a compromise with them in not working as much may be the best course of action in finding your highest level of happiness and satisfaction.

If you don't make time for yourself to recharge and unwind, your body or mind will force it to sooner or later. That won't be nearly as fun as you deciding how to do it yourself. Make time to play a little bit. You'll find yourself flowing through stressful times much more easily.

Chapter 8
Visualization

I challenge you to start seeing and saying yourself happy.

Many times in life we are down or discouraged, in part because we look at ourselves that way. We see ourselves in our mind's eye as a down and out person. It's natural to be down occasionally, but staying there is another matter. You will never be able to live happily and contented unless you see yourself being able to do it.

Visualization is a process by which you picture in your mind what you want to occur before it happens. To visualize yourself is to get a mental picture of who you want to be and to see yourself doing what you want to do. Many people roll their eyes at this concept. Others label it "New Age," or "Mystical." Neither is true.

Thousands of years ago God promised Abraham he would father a child with his wife Sarah. Abraham was nearly 100 years old, and Sarah was 90. Both of them thought it was ridiculous. But God told him to go outside at night and look up at the clear, starry sky. He told him his offspring would be as many as all those stars he couldn't even count. It eventually happened. (Gen. 17:15-19)

Abraham just needed to get the picture in his mind, seeing himself with that many descendants.

This process of visualization can help in your quest for a satisfying, happy life. First and foremost, attaining goals in life is highly satisfying. When you achieve you feel great. Seeing yourself being what you want to be enables you to more easily believe that you will become what you want to become. The more often you practice this process, the more solid and clear the picture becomes in your mind. The more clearly you see yourself attaining your goals, the greater your chances become of actually doing so.

When I was learning my martial art of Hapkido, as I rose in rank nearing the time for my black belt test, my instructor ordered my belt with my name on it. He placed it in the glass case at the counter I walked by every time I came into the academy. Many times I would be there alone. I would stare into the case at my name embroidered in gold on that black belt. I could have touched it, but I never did. Mentally I saw myself receiving it from my instructor's hand at the conclusion of my test, him tying it around my waist for me, which is only done for black belts. I also saw myself wearing it as instructor for the class. He knew letting me see it constantly would push me toward excellence. He was right.

It's been said that the great movie star, former governor of California and champion body builder, Arnold Schwarzenegger, was asked once how he became the greatest body builder of his time. "Simple," he was reported to have said. "I developed a picture in my mind of me winning and becoming the greatest; then I just lived my life into this picture." He visualized himself as the best, and he became the best. When he moved into acting, he said he wanted to be one of the greatest action stars in films. He began to see himself becoming a huge star. You know what happened.

You may not want to be a star; it doesn't matter. Seeing yourself rising, growing, and achieving will help you get closer and closer to whatever it is you want to attain. When you begin to envision yourself happy and at ease mentally, the rest of you will gravitate in that direction.

Sticks and Stones

Closely related to how you see yourself is what you say about yourself.

People go about their lives saying defeating things about themselves every day. It has become so ingrained in our world that we don't even notice that we do it. The power of our words is closely related to the power of visualization. Whether you realize it or not, when you say something demeaning about yourself your mind hears it. Then it processes it away, banking up information supporting the notion that you are defeated, unable, and unsuccessful. Thankfully the opposite is also true. When your mind is routinely hearing, *"I can, I will, it's possible,"* then before long you'll start saying, *"I did"* and *"I have it!"*

Start today being more mindful of your words especially in reference to yourself and your abilities and attributes.

Think how much more satisfying your life could be a year from now if you did nothing differently than to start saying five positive things about yourself and your future every day. I challenge you to start seeing and saying yourself happy. When you start believing yourself, what you see and what you hear, your life will start moving in that direction.

It's not all about where you're going. Your today benefits from positive affirmation, too. Everyday life is happier, more refreshing when you see yourself in a positive light; when you are saying good things about your world and your situation. Remind yourself of the importance of this by writing down positive affirmations on paper or your computer so you will see them each day. Review them every day until it starts becoming part of you. Then, find other ones to write down, growing your mental picture of yourself. When you believe you achieve. And as it's believed the Ford Motor

Company founder Henry Ford said, "If you believe you can, or you believe you can't, you're right."

"The tongue has the power of life and death ... ." (Prov. 18:21) Clearly, it is not a new theory that what we say is of great importance. How much improved would our lives be if we spoke more positively about ourselves and our situation? The trouble is when you talk to someone about speaking positively about their life and the effect it has, and they reply, "Oh yeah! You've got to speak good things and not all that bad junk about yourself." But they're the ones doing it wrong all the time. We have a tendency to think the advice is for the other guy. Remember, you don't know what you don't know. For example, If you've never seen clearly then you don't know your vision is obscured. We should reflect on our own words and actions, and look honestly and without reservation at what we *actually* do or say not just what we *think* we do or say, and if need be, adjust it accordingly to what we want in our lives.

You may agree, but now find yourself thinking, "I don't know about all this positive stuff." It's ok. I would simply encourage you to start trying it little by little. What do you have to lose, negativity? So what? You may gain a new and fresh perspective on life. And one thing has a tendency to lead to another. You may find yourself more encouraged, positive and generally happier in everyday life.

Chapter 9
Control

"No" is a perfectly legitimate answer to a question.

C ontrol is something we always want to be in and, at the same time, free from. Control can be a good thing and a bad thing too. It depends a little on your point of view. This is a place where peace and joy inside you can spring a leak. Too little control results in chaos, while too much control is akin to being in prison.

Do you like being in control? What do you like to control—yourself, other people, circumstances, and conditions? Many people want to control others, but usually never want others to have control over them. Most of the controlling people I have met in my life appear not to know, or believe, that they are, in fact, very controlling. Others know it but see no harm in it, telling themselves it's just their way of being shrewd and knowing how to get what they want. Here we will look at aspects of control and how they affect your life positively and negatively.

To begin with, trying to be in control of situations you are in can have a strong negative effect on your life. It's exhausting trying to maintain any control over others. Working to get people to think your way, or manipulating relationships for your own good, are exercises that will never pay dividends compared to the investments you have in them. The constant drain of energy on a person who is trying to maintain conditions of a relationship to suit their own purposes will cost them dearly, and the rewards are never worth it. Ultimately, you can't have much control over people or relationships anyway, you only have control over yourself. Often we lie to ourselves thinking if we can just get them thinking this or that, then we can keep getting this or that. But it will always end in an energy drain rather than an energy gain.

The path to contentment is releasing any thought of manipulation. This is difficult to handle if you are one who has operated this way a long time, or if you grew up in that kind of environment. Giving up control over others' actions is liberating, though. When you finally realize that you're not going to be responsible for another person's actions or attitudes, then you can finally live in freedom. The joy of knowing that you are not responsible for the outcome of a situation or how people feel about it or you, is incomparable. That joy comes in not trying to convince people. It's liberating living your life with truth and freedom passing on that attitude, then allowing them to do whatever they choose with it. That is total freedom from false responsibility.

Equally important is not allowing anyone to control us. That is not to say that we don't submit to another's will. Part of having a great marriage is putting your will aside and submitting to theirs out of love, for instance. This is not control happening to you, it's self control. You will, however, always have people at various places and times in your life, attempting to place some sort of control on you. You must be the one who decides if that control will be allowed or not.

Pressures come from all arenas in life. People will always pull on you in one direction or another. For your own good and happiness, you will need to limit the power this has over you. You see, you won't be able to always say "yes" to everyone.

They may be well intentioned and the cause may be noble, but you can't do what everybody wants you to do. You must learn to control you. Allowing others to decide things like where you'll be and what to do will be like pouring your hard won happiness down the drain.

Take everything into consideration, then decide for yourself what you will or won't do, or what your opinion is or isn't. If you don't have control over you, others will seize that control. It may not be malicious, but it's just human nature. We have a tendency to fill voids. For a person to be happy and content, they need to be the one who decides how and when to submit to others and when to gently repel the external forces on their lives that would attempt to commandeer the control they have over themselves.

The power of "No"

For those of us who want to be nice to people, it's often difficult when we're asked to take on some sort of responsibility to simply say no. "No" is a perfectly legitimate answer to a question. In today's society we're almost afraid to say the word to someone because we might offend them. Further, we're told if we offend people then that is a negative trait to have. If we are negative then we must be wrong because being positive is good; therefore, we should never tell people "no."

I believe that kind of thinking is ridiculous. More and more people are complaining nowadays, saying, "I'm just so busy"; "I feel stressed out all the time"; "There just never seems to be any down time anymore." These complaints, and many others, are absolutely legitimate. People who have a few years under their belt talk of days when families used to sit on the porch in the evenings, have picnics, and watch television together. "Times were simpler back then," we often hear, which is true, to a large extent.

With progress has come pressure. Have you seen some of those old movies made in the 1940s or so, where they hailed all the technological advances being made, like the clothes washer and dryer? These devices were designed to give the homemaker much more leisure time. However, when we learned that we had more time on our hands, we surmised that we could accomplish more if we worked on something else while a machine was doing something for us. Now work output doubled, and people soon realized we all had more time on our hands. They began to feel comfortable asking more of others because we could do more with our time. A hundred years ago no one would think of asking you to travel several miles two or three times a week for a meeting. That was considered too long of a journey. But with cars, today you're expected to do that all the time. And to be honest, I don't see that trend slowing down any time soon.

This is why we need to learn the *art* of saying "No." The "art," you may ask? Yes, because if you're anything like me, you may need help with how you sound and, perhaps, also how you appear when you say no. I'm rather somber looking all the time, for instance, and have to work at not looking like I'm upset to other people. Combine that with an answer that may be taken negatively, and you could have a personal relations train wreck.

How do you say no and not cause tension? When I feel cornered into doing something someone asks, but I know I've mentally left time open for fun or relaxation, I tell them I have an appointment at that time (as we discussed in Chapter 7). As I mentioned, you do not have to explain what your appointments are regardless of whether it's a doctor's appointment or an appointment to have coffee and relax. That's irrelevant. It's *your* appointment. Also, if you're put on the spot, but you don't know if you are free at that time, tell the person you'll check your schedule and get back with them. Remember, there's an art to saying "No." You will have to practice it to get good at it.

Another tip is when someone asks you what you have going on at such and such time on a certain day; don't automatically say "Nothing" or "I don't know." Ask them a question like, "What do you have in mind?" or "What's going on with you then?" By asking a question, you have immediately leveled the playing field, or perhaps slanted it in your favor slightly.

I don't want to make this sound like a strategy for war to defeat an enemy; however, you *are* defending something: your time, your schedule, and your sanity. Remember, if they ask what you're doing Friday at four, for instance, and you say "nothing," then in reality there will be almost zero chance that you are going to end up saying "no" to what they ask, assuming you may want to.

My advice is to try to avoid control, both of you and by you. It's tempting to want to get control over people and situations. We think that by doing so we will have things the way we want them. It's an empty promise. The energy expenditure will be too great. The stress of trying to manage it will outweigh any benefit we might receive from it. Everything will unravel anyway. Additionally, gently avoid coming under the control of others at all costs. When you feel controlled by another, animosity will begin to build. This will eventually destroy your peace and, quite possibly, the relationship you have with the person who is exerting the control.

Chapter 10
Aging

*You can't necessarily *be* anything you want, but you can *become* anything you dedicate yourself to.*

T hings change all the time. We know this is true, yet we seem to be caught off guard every time things in our lives change. As we go through life many conditions of our lives change as we age. I'm not necessarily referring to becoming an old person here, although that's part of it, too. Aging is simply progressing in time through life, and nearly everything will change along that path. As we grow older from our teens into adulthood, we experience various changes from physical aspects to the responsibilities that are required. Moving from middle age into our later years we again experience alterations in many of the same areas of life but, perhaps, differently. If you're going to enjoy your life, you must embrace these things as they begin to happen.

As I mentioned earlier, we know that change is usually difficult to deal with. Aging, however, is a continual process of change happening in life. To be happy with life means to be happy with where you are, not limiting your ability to enjoy life to only when things come into a certain state of condition. You see, those conditions will eventually change, and, if you're not prepared, your happiness will go right out the window. The sooner in life we can come to terms with the notion that as we age life will be different, the sooner we overcome the anxiety over seeing those things change and stop trying to hold on to the conditions as they were.

I believe one of the keys to being able to embrace and keep contentment in life as we get older is having an early awareness of these things. Knowing what to expect brings comfort into situations. Any time we can see what's up the path ahead of us, it's easier to take the next steps along that path without fear of the unknown. Then, if we can begin to embrace the concept that as we move through life many of the traits or conditions of our lives will definitely change, then we will always be more prepared for them and as a result, can live with more surety and comfort daily.

With this preparation for changes in mind, let's look at a few areas of life that might otherwise try to throw a wet blanket on our everyday contentment.

Your wants may change

What you enjoy may change. This might not seem to be an issue to you as you read it, but it can cause you a little grief when it happens. I'm not talking about one devastating event that shatters your life; it's more in reference to the phrase, "death by a thousand small cuts."

It happened to me this way: Since I was very young, I have been involved in the outdoors, especially hunting. I've always loved hunting, shooting, and being in the woods. As I matured, I expanded my scope of hunting pursuits to include many species and the various times of year to hunt them. I began going to other states to hunt wild turkeys (a passion of mine) for more opportunities to hunt them. I became involved in a call making company. I loved it. I lived and breathed it. And in my own little world, I became known for it. I still love it.

My Dad and I hunted together a lot. But over time I began to notice his reluctance to go out on rather cold days. He gradually became less interested in hunting, and would rarely go without me. I became perplexed over his lack of enthusiasm. When I mentioned it he would say, "I just don't really want to go anymore." I was bewildered, and couldn't possibly see why he wouldn't want to get out there. I was eating eat up.

Several years ago, I became involved with martial arts, and as I have a tendency to do, I loved it very much, too. Over time, I noticed that my drive and passion to get out into the woods wasn't what it used to be. I began to make excuses to stay home rather than get out into the cold. As I said before, it may not sound like much to you, but this was who I had become. I couldn't understand why I didn't care as much anymore, and it actually bothered me. My family also questioned me about it. It bothered me that people thought something was wrong. Then I heard a wise man say, "Your life will change over time. Don't let it bother you when things you used to love, you don't want that much anymore." I began to realize that I had placed expectations upon myself about who I was and what I was. I finally began to reason with myself that I did all that because I enjoyed it, right? Well, why shouldn't I enjoy myself by not going when I don't want to go as well?

I found myself more involved in martial arts and less and less in hunting. I still love to hunt, and I love martial arts. Now I understand what Dad was going through. I wish I could go back and be more understanding. But now I do what makes me happy at the time, and I don't try to keep up with what I *used to* enjoy.

Don't allow your own past, or other's opinions pressure you. You know what you like. You know best what makes you happy. Many people get hung up on losing desire over a goal they once had. There again, you may have set that goal at a time when you were absolutely obsessed with that activity. As you move through life and become interested in other pursuits, past goals may not seem nearly as important anymore. Guilt may try to creep in concerning goals that you didn't achieve. You may question yourself as to why you didn't persist and achieve your goal. You must resist this line of thought and adopt a different train of thought. Remind yourself that it doesn't matter anymore, and you can choose what you want in life.

Don't concern yourself with goals you used to have when you've moved on to other pursuits. It's not a failure, just a normal change in life. Embrace it.

Your situation may change

As you move forward in time, you inevitably are going to encounter changes—some expected, some unexpected. Early on you have ancestors, possibly several, and no descendants for instance. Later, if you have children, you find yourself with more descendants and fewer ancestors, until you finally arrive at the place where you *are* the ancestor and the rest are descendants.

The death of family members, specifically grandparents and parents, not only present great changes to cope with, but also change our situation within the family structure, further changing our situation with more variables to deal with. We must understand that as we age, many changes like this are inevitable. Again, early detection is very helpful. Knowing these things may come—some definitely will come—helps retain a sense of peace and stability in our lives when that time arrives.

I remember sitting down with Bobbi when our two daughters were teenagers, and beginning to talk with her about the inevitable time when they would be gone from our home. She stared at me with a rather blank look on her face and said, "I've never thought past getting married and raising a family." We began immediately to have more dialogue about what our lives might look like without children at home. She began to get more and more vision of us living as empty nesters.

Looking back, it seems like we just blinked our eyes and that day came. Bobbi was much better prepared to handle it because of our preparation and discussions. Understand that your life situations will change. Flow with these alterations. Find the things to rejoice about in them.

Your body will change

As long as you live, you are aging. I am a firm believer in beating back the process; however, all you can do is prolong the inevitable. Many of us start putting on weight soon after we get out of high school or college. Marriage seems to have this effect on many of us, too. It's needless, yet common. Middle age also comes with its own little surprises, like wrinkles, graying hair, and a little sagging in places that didn't sag before.

It's funny how when you're young you don't think it's going to happen to you, as if you will somehow magically escape what every other human experiences. Yet it happens. The key, again, is early detection. We must anticipate the process before it actually begins, so we're not blindsided. These changes are absolutely natural and should not be looked at as something bad. Relish the age you are now. We're usually not as rash in decision making as we were when we were young. Think about all of the good things about where you are in life. Some things are better with age, as with good wine. You learn, as we have discussed earlier, to be content with who you are in life.

Sexuality can be something also that gets better with age, contrary to what young people think. There is a comfort in having a mate whom you know so well that you just can't find in a shorter term relationship. My wife and I have been married for 35 years, and every aspect of our relationship is better today than ever. And I mean *every* aspect, if you know what I mean. But we've worked at it; not taking our marriage for granted. The old saying is true: "Anything worth doing is worth doing well."

Some folks are really hung up on wrinkles and grey hair. My advice is to do what makes you happy. If you want to color your hair, do it. Use Botox? If you can, and it makes you happy, go for it.

Don't let someone else decide for you what will please you. That's sure to keep you from being happy and satisfied with your life.

You may be surprised at what you can actually do. You get weaker with age. Muscles don't respond as well as in your youth. Test your limits sometimes. You might surprise yourself with what you can accomplish if you dedicate yourself to it. Don't be afraid to change your career later in life either. Colonel Sanders was in his 60s when he started Kentucky Fried Chicken. It's never too late to do what you want to do. Remember, you can't necessarily *be* anything you want, but you can *become* anything you dedicate yourself to.

Chapter 11
Spirituality

"Empty your cup that it may be filled." — *Bruce Lee*

To me, and to many of the wisest and most successful people I know, we gain one of the deepest satisfactions and peace in life through the cultivation of personal spirituality. I believe we are two-part creatures: physical and spiritual. You may not put much stock in such things, or you may have deeply held beliefs and practices of your own, but I urge you to read to the end. Hear out the words that follow, then use Bruce Lee's approach to keeping what is useful ... and make it distinctly your own.

The main reason I believe that cultivation of the spiritual aspect of our lives is so important can be summed up in a quote I read in Joseph Cardillo's book by Ram Dass: "We are not physical beings having a spiritual experience. We are spiritual beings having a physical experience." (Cardillo 2003, Dass)

We know about the physical part, as we deal with it every day. It's easy to come to terms with its existence. It's always in our face. It *is* our face. I believe, however, that true happiness in life can only be experienced when we nurture the other part of our being—the spirit. Now, don't hear what I'm not saying. All of the principles and techniques I've presented work, I believe, regardless of your beliefs or lack thereof concerning spiritual matters. But, to truly have happiness within, the whole man (or woman), the spiritual and the physical, must be nourished, exercised, healed and whole.

When referring to the spiritual dimension, some may think I'm referring to only a person's religious beliefs. While that's true, I'm also referring to the inner man, which is the part of us that makes us who we are, apart from the physical body. Our spirit is what makes us the individual we are. Spirit contains qualities that can't truly be defined within the physical. When we look at someone in the physical we can describe them based on what we see with the eyes; for example, noting, "He sure is tall"; "She has beautiful hair"; or, "He doesn't look his age." With the spirit, however, we may still "see things" about a person, just not exactly with the eyes. For example, we might comment, "I get a good feeling when we talk"; "She just has a way about her!" Or, on the other side of the coin, "When we get together something just doesn't feel right." These are similar observations made not with the physical, but the spiritual.

In our journey toward happiness, we must learn to listen with our spirit, just as we would see with our eyes, listen with our ears, or feel with our hands in the physical. As with many other things, this may not come as easily as it sounds. Just like any skill, it has to be cultivated. We can train ourselves to be more in tune with our spirit. Just as a sedentary person, who hardly moves their body all day can't possibly expect to suddenly run, jump, or swim to any extent, a person who has neglected the spiritual part of life can't expect to immediately see, feel and hear with their spirit. The good news is that anyone, who is willing, can grow themselves spiritually. As with bodily exercise, it will take time, effort and persistence; and changes will come.

We can't expect to walk around in life at peace with ourselves and generally happy if we only focus on one part of our two-part being. I think it's interesting that when reading through the Bible, when referring to a person's happiness, or lack thereof, it frequently uses the word "joy" instead. I believe this is because the physical person alone can be relatively contented, thus denoting the feeling of happiness. When the inner man, known as our spirit, however, is experiencing the same kind of peace and contentment, the two combined bring about a higher level of well being that can only be adequately described as joy.

Without explaining the difference, you can experience the difference by saying the word "happy" and then saying the word "joyful." You see? Joy is happiness of the physical *and* the spiritual. It is a much deeper level of happiness. The effect on a person is greater than the sum of the two together. Instead of *adding* to your level of well being, the two parts of your person happy and whole together, will *multiply* your well being. This is why we shouldn't neglect our spiritual person. We have too much to lose.

The voice within

Many times in the course of life we just know something we were supposed to do or say or what *not* to do or say. Because your spirit is not physical, it doesn't have a mouth for talking. It will, however, talk to you. We just need to learn to understand how to hear it. Some people call it intuition. When we feel something inside we need to learn to trust that feeling. That is our spirit expressing to our flesh that something's not right. It may, at other times, be telling us when to act. As with so many other experiences in life, if it's beneficial for us, it may not be easy. Hearing your spirit man will require patience and persistence. If you invest in listening, though, you will uncover a valuable resource that can add to the happiness and richness of your life. That little voice can keep you out of trouble or it may lead you to opportunities you weren't initially aware of.

Your spirit records things throughout your life that your mind may have ignored or forgotten. Then it will notify you of problems about to arise when your mind may be charging ahead. In time, you will have a more complete system of information at your disposal to draw from because the two parts of your being will be working in unison.

The Great Spirit

The other side of spirituality includes our belief in a spirit greater than ourselves. With due respect to all readers, I urge you to believe in God. I am not implying that if you don't you can't be happy or that you are in any way inferior. What I am saying is that in my own life, belief in God has made a great difference. Actually, it has made all the difference. As a Christian, my belief centers on Jesus dying for the forgiveness of sins. That includes my sin. Confidence in that atonement made for me allows me to face life, and death, with a freedom I would not otherwise have.

I won't rant and rave to you about your religion, or lack thereof. I would simply encourage you to open yourself to the possibility of a creator, a spirit, greater than yourself. One that would like to talk to your spirit and have you talk to Him. I believe this is a path to deeper fulfillment, joy and satisfaction in life. Just try it, see what happens. You are under no pressure or obligation. Just be open to the voice you hear within, and remain open to yourself about that voice. In the words of Bruce Lee: "Empty your cup that it may be filled."

Chapter 12
Finances

The *love of* money is the root of all evil. (1 Tim. 6:10)

Money; no one seems to make enough. Everyone needs just a little bit more. Happiness today seems to be linked with having plenty of money. However, rich people are known to commit suicide regularly. How can that be if lots of money will bring lots of happiness? People who are wealthy still deal with family problems, depression, job loss, and health issues. Many folks with lots of money still end up in debt problems and filing for bankruptcy. Now, I'm not going to tell you that being able to pay your bills on time and purchasing whatever you need is not better than living with lack all the time.

Money can solve some problems. It just won't solve all your problems.

Understanding Money

All my life I've heard people say, "Money is the root of all evil." It has become a "sinister" thing that we all want, but we still feel bad about admitting that we do. One reason for this is that the quote about money is incorrect. It comes from the Bible in 1

Timothy 6:10, which states, "The *love* of money is the root of all evil." You see, money is neither good nor bad. It simply is. What you do with it, and what you think about it is what's important. I am confident of this, if you love money, happiness will slip from your grasp like a greased icicle.

Money is a tool that will enable you to do many things, but making your life happy is not one of them. You must learn to be happy first and then money can simply be a nice addition to your life. Trying to do it the other way around is like trying to put the cart in front of the horse. In the same way, we get our lives into a place of normal everyday contentment and joy, then the finances come behind us, adding to the happiness that's already in place.

Contentment

What I've been saying is that you won't finally be content only when you have a certain amount of money. You must learn contentment whether you're rich or poor. The Apostle Paul said, it this way: "I have learned to be content whatever the circumstances." (Phil. 4:11) He experienced plenty and lack, health and illness, prison and freedom. It can be done. Even in poverty you can learn to be content. The key is in the peace of mind that comes from knowing you are doing the best you can do with what you have now. Being smart with the money at your disposal is very satisfying. In addition, you never know who may be around you who holds the keys to your financial future. If you are known for spending recklessly, that person may overlook you when opportunity arises. Learning to live your life within the boundaries of your financial circumstances, with contentment, is your foundation for a happy financial life no matter how much you get.

Gain control

We who have found ourselves in financial distress, at times, have learned something about money. You have to control your money or it will control you. There is a slippery quality to having excess funds. In case you haven't noticed, it seems to spend easier and quicker than it comes in; it's a lot like diet and calories. You have to exercise very strenuously, depending on your weight, gender and other factors, for maybe an hour to burn off the same amount of calories in a doughnut that you will eat in just two minutes or less, for instance. By the same token, you can go out for dinner, a movie and shopping, and spend possibly two to five days worth of income. It goes away easily. It earns hard.

If you gain control over where it goes and how much of it goes, then financial peace is within your grasp. If not, then you will become enslaved to it. You will find yourself doing nothing but trying to get more in order to keep up with the draining of money going out. I'm not against debt completely; however, as it says in scripture, "The borrower is servant to the lender." (Prov. 22:7) If you enter into debt you, in essence, become a servant to another. A servant's primary concerns are the desires of their master. That has a negative effect on our happiness. The more servitude you have to endure, the less happiness you will have. The more mastery you have, the more happiness will be at your disposal. Freedom is fun. Enslavement is not. Gaining control may take some time. Don't be discouraged by that. Allow for time. Expect it. Then you won't be dismayed over that aspect and lose hope.

Set yourself goals and rejoice over each step toward it. Remember, too, getting closer to your goal is progress. Look at *moving* toward your goal as success, not only just *reaching* it. Every step in the direction of financial control is success. See it that way. Celebrate the small steps to keep enthusiasm high, and that will build momentum. Happiness will find you when you are in the driver's seat, not your money.

Giving

The happiest people I know are people who give of their substance regularly. You know the old saying, "What goes around, comes around." This is more than just an old tale. I have found this is true not only financially, but in all aspects of life. The main reason many people don't believe that is because often there is some time that will elapse between the "going around" and the "coming around." To add to the frustration, the time in between isn't always the same. When we don't see it happen right away, we begin to doubt whether it's true or not. Scripture says a man reaps what he sows. (Gal. 6:7) Giving regularly will position you to receiving regularly, provided you are patient, and don't stop prematurely before you see it working.

There is also tremendous satisfaction gained in helping a person or cause with your supply. Stingy people disagree, citing the fact that they had to earn theirs so everyone else does too. These folks, I have found, are generally unhappy and stressed. There is false hope in selfishness. It promises a lot, but never delivers. And yet, people will keep believing the lying voice of selfishness and continue hoarding every meager morsel for themselves in the hopes of having more.

Remember reading that continuing to do the same thing while expecting different results is insane? (Einstein) Do you want something different financially? Start doing something different with your finances. If you've never been a giver, start now. Start slowly, but consistently. Find a worthy cause or ministry and begin. Giving is one of the noblest and most selfless things you can do. Try it, wait with patience, and discover satisfaction that can't be obtained otherwise.

Chapter 13
Exceptions

"If you correct your mind, the rest of your life will fall into place." — *Lao Tzu*

I want to make something clear here at the end. Those suffering with clinical diagnosis of depression or mental disorders should never take my suggestions as a cure for their problems. Everything I've written is to help increase your happiness with your everyday world. After all, your life is mainly comprised of the everyday routine with its everyday experiences. This is where you can make the greatest difference in your life. There are times that will come along and knock us down, such as the death of a spouse, child, or parent; receiving the news of a dreaded disease from the doctor, divorce, and so on.

When these events occur, you aren't' going to be happy. It's ok not to be. Grieving *must* take place when you experience tragic loss. We are created to do so. Sometimes the only way to get to the other side of something is *through* it. Please understand, there is no false guilt, no pressure, no advice even, telling you to just cheer up and be happy when your world has been torn apart.

Crying is ok, too, for women and men. Do not listen to

someone who tells you simply to look at the bright side. Not yet, anyway. In devastating circumstances, there has to be time for healing. Just like with a severe injury, you can't go straight to therapy and immediately back to work. There must be healing and recovery. Then you can begin to think about enjoying life again.

As referenced earlier in Ecc. 3:1, King Solomon, the wisest man to ever live, wrote, "There is a time and a place for everything." When difficult times subside, and they will, you will have the rest of your life to enjoy everyday happiness.

Live life the way you decide. Take advice, weigh it out, then make your decisions. Don't let naysayers deride you. Be confident, but not arrogant. Let the screamers scream, but be unaffected. Don't panic, ever. Stay calm and move forward. Enjoy the small things and find the good where you can. Look again, a little harder, and find the good where you can. There is usually some good that gets overlooked. That will be yours to enjoy alone, away from the stampeding masses.

"If you correct your mind, the rest of your life will fall into place." — Lao Tzu

Farewell.

Thoughts

My personal thoughts, and favorite quotes and phrases.

~ You can't be anything you want, but you can *become* anything you want.
~ Don't hear what I'm not saying.
~ If you correct your mind, the rest of your life will fall into place. (Lao Tzu)
~ The secret of your future is hidden in your daily routine.
~ Remember to always be wherever you are.
~ *This* is the day the Lord has made. I *will* rejoice and be glad *in it. (Ps. 118:24)*
~ "No" is a perfectly legitimate answer.
~ There's no time like the present. There's no present like the time.
~ The best exercise routine is the one you'll *do.*
~ The more the words, the less the meaning. (Ecc. 6:11)
~ A journey of a thousand miles begins with a single step. (Lao Tzu)
~ You don't know what you don't know.
~ Focus on what you've *got*, instead of what you've *not.*
~ Fall down seven times, get up eight.

- I will actively respect the sentiments of others, even when I disagree with them.
- Never fear changing how you are, even when you've always been some other way because of what people think.
- People may be saying something bad about you right now, and you don't know it. So relax.
- How I respond to something is much more important than what actually happens to me.
- The Bible says "Fear not" 365 times; once for every day of the year.
- Fear cripples.
- Fear immobilizes.
- Nothing is ever as bad as it first seems.
- Assess threats properly.
- Never meet force head on. Redirect energy into your favor.
- A day of favor is worth a lifetime of labor. (Murdock)
- You don't need everyone liking you, just the right person liking you.
- There is a time and a season for every activity under heaven. (Ecc. 3:1)
- All have sinned and fall short of the glory of God. (Rom. 3:23)
- If you keep on doing what you're doing, you'll keep getting what you're getting.
- Doing the same thing over and over, but expecting different results, is the definition of insanity. (Albert Einstein)
- "Your actions speak so loudly I can't hear with your saying." (Unknown)
- There is great power in forgiving someone who has wronged you.
- If you don't forgive, you can't go to heaven. (Jesus, Mat. 6:15)
- Life is made up of "right nows."
- You must *start* on the path. Think what you will, and prepare how you will. But you must start.

~ The best teachers are those who show you where to look, but don't tell you what to see.
~ Don't presume to know what's going to happen. Empty your mind to flow with what happens.
~ You have two ears and one mouth. Listen twice as much as you speak.
~ Never speak evil of the ruler of your people. (Acts 23:5, Exo. 22:28)
~ Live in *today*. Yesterday is only a memory, never to return. Tomorrow is only in your imagination.
~ What you were in your past doesn't have to affect what you are now, or what you will be.
~ "Can't" is a four-letter word.
~ Picture what you want, then live in to that picture.
~ God showed Abraham all the stars and said that was the number of offspring Abraham would have. Abraham was almost 100 years old and childless at the time. (Gen. 15:5)
~ God first, spouse second, family third, everything else after that.
~ Enjoy the everyday. This is what your life is primarily made up of, not the Christmases, birthdays and vacations. If you can't enjoy the *normal* days, you can't enjoy your life. That's mostly what it's made of.
~ Beware of waiting until the time is exactly right. It never is.
~ You will always have bills to pay.
~ Forgive *yourself*.
~ Get over yourself.
~ Believe in yourself.
~ Don't think *too* highly of yourself.
~ It's *your* time. *You* decide what to do with it.
~ If someone doesn't like you, don't worry about it; that's just the one you found out about.
~ Strive to extract all pleasure you can from *whatever* you're doing.

- ~ Mercy before judgment.
- ~ "If you think you can, or you think you can't ... you're right." (Henry Ford)
- ~ When people treat you badly, it's *their* problem.
- ~ "If you've done your best, what do you have to fear?" (Bruce Lee, 1975)
- ~ "Be like water." (Lee, 1975)
- ~ Don't presume before what may happen. React to what is.
- ~ Most things you worry about will never happen anyway.
- ~ "If you think about something too long you may never get it done." — Bruce Lee
- ~ "Do not worry." (Jesus, Mat. 6:25)
- ~ "Empty your cup that it may be filled." (Lee, 2000)

Bibliography and References

Television evangelist Dr. Mike Murdock is the founder and senior pastor of the Wisdom Center ministry based in Fort Worth, Texas. References to his work come from his numerous books and various television appearances.

Bruce Lee (November 27, 1940 - July 20, 1973) actor, director, philosopher and martial-arts expert born Lee Jun Fan in San Francisco, California; www.brucelee.com/legacy; "Tao of Jeet Kune Do" published posthumously (1975); "Striking Thoughts: Bruce Lee's Wisdom for Daily Living" (2000) edited by John Little.

Joe Hyams, author of "Zen in the Martial Arts" (1979).

Biblical references taken from the New International Version unless otherwise noted: Proverbs 23:7 (King James Version); Matthew 6:25,27; Ecclesiastes 3:1; Rom. 12:18; John 8:7; Prov. 12:16; Mark 6:31; Gen. 17:15-19; 1 Timothy 6:10; Philippians 4:11; Prov. 22:7; Gal. 6:7

Joseph Cardillo, PhD, is a best-selling author in the fields of health, mind-body-spirit, and psychology. "Be like Water: Practical Wisdom from the Martial Arts" (2003)

Franklin Delano Roosevelt (January 30, 1882 – April 12, 1945), commonly known by his initials FDR, was an American statesman and political leader who served as the 32nd President of the United States, who served four terms from March 1933 to his death in April 1945.

Lao Tzu, quoted " The journey of a thousand miles begins with a single step." Tao Te Ching Daodejing, or Dao De Jing, also Laozi; a Chinese classic text, according to tradition, was written in about the 6th century BC by the sage Laozi (or Lao Tzu)

Francois Henri "Jack" LaLanne (September 26, 1914 – January 23, 2011); radio and television personality; an American fitness, exercise, and nutritional expert and motivational speaker.

Arnold Schwarzenegger (July 30, 1947); an Austrian-born American actor, producer, activist, businessman, investor, writer, philanthropist, former professional bodybuilder, and 38th Governor of California (2003-2011).

Henry Ford (July 30, 1863 – April 7, 1947); founder of the Ford Motor Company, and sponsor of the development of the assembly line technique of mass production.

Ram Dass (born Richard Alpert; April 6, 1931); an American contemporary spiritual teacher and the author

William Cowper's poem, "The Task" (1785) "The Timepiece (Book II, lines 285-6); "Variety is the very spice of life, That gives it all its flavor."

About the Author:
Steve Haverly

Steve is a husband, father, and grandfather, and has served for 31 years as a career firefighter. He has experienced the highs and lows in life like everyone else. In the midst of a great marriage, wonderful children, and a good job, he was missing out on much of the peace and contentment that could be his, so he began to analyze his own life. He found he couldn't wait for the big events in life to make him happy. He needed to make it happen right away.

A process of understanding began through which he discovered bits of wisdom that revealed how to develop and retain a higher level of happiness, peace, and joy in everyday life.

Steve has drawn from experiences in fire service leadership, martial arts, church government service, and mentors he has sought out. He wrote this book to help lead you to a happier, more joyful and satisfied life. You can learn to be happy right now.

Printed in the United States
By Bookmasters